Investigating the
BOSTON MARATHON
BOMBINGS

GREG BALDINO

Rosen
YA
New York

Published in 2018 by The Rosen Publishing Group, Inc.
29 East 21st Street, New York, NY 10010

Library of Congress Cataloging-in-Publication Data

Names: Baldino, Greg, author.
Title: Investigating the Boston Marathon bombings / Greg Baldino.
Description: First edition. | New York, NY : Rosen Publishing Group, Inc.,
   2018. | Series: Terrorism in the 21st century: causes and effects |
   Includes bibliographical references and index. | Audience: Grades 7-12.
Identifiers: LCCN 2016059472 | ISBN 9781508174578 (library bound)
Subjects: LCSH: Boston Marathon Bombing, Boston, Mass., 2013Juvenile
   literature. | Terrorism–Massachusetts–Boston–Juvenile literature.
Classification: LCC HV6432.8 .B35 2018 | DDC 363.325/97964252–dc23
LC record available at https://lccn.loc.gov/2016059472

Manufactured in China

On the cover: A man lays flowers down at a memorial for victims of the Boston Marathon bombings in 2013.

Contents

Introduction

You've been working toward this for a long time. Today is the day of the Boston Marathon, an event you have trained hard for. When you first started, you could run for about half an hour before getting tired, but you kept at it until it stopped being hard. Every week, alternating days off and days running, the amount of distance you could comfortably run got longer and longer. In the past week, you've actually run fewer miles, so you would be rested and prepared to run the 26 miles (42 kilometers).

Along the race route, family and friends have waited to see you run past and cheer you on. This is a momentous event! When the race is over, the bib pinned to your shirt with your number will become a treasured memento.

As the campus of Boston College passes by, you start to slow down. But you were expecting this; you knew that meant your body was beginning to break down fat cells for energy instead of fast-burning carbohydrates. So you slow down to let your metabolism switch gears.

Now, the last mile is underway. You're almost to the finish line! The breeze coming off the nearby Charles River is refreshing. All around you are other runners. Some of them are running their first marathon, just like you. Others have run many before. There are so many different people, older and younger, men and women, different races and religions from all over the world.

Then, you hear a noise: a thunderous crash from up ahead. Suddenly the people ahead of you are turning and running the opposite way. This makes no sense. What is happening? What is going on?

The Boston Marathon bombings were the second major terrorist attack on American soil after the September 11 attacks in 2001. Both the attacks and the responses to them were very different, and those differences tell us a lot about how terrorism in America changed over those twelve years.

Tens of thousands of men and women come from all over the world to run in the Boston Marathon each year.

One of the differences between these two acts of terrorism is that the September 11 attacks were planned and carried out by the terrorist organization al-Qaeda, while the attack in Boston was conducted by just two people—the brothers Dzhokhar and Tamerlan Tsarnaev—who were not affiliated with any group.

Also, while the targets of the September 11 attacks had been the World Trade Center and the Pentagon during the regular workday, the people attacked in Boston were gathered on the streets in large groups. People from all around the world were either running or watching, and the participants were in a heightened state from running so many miles. However, one of the biggest differences was the response to the attacks. After the bombing, the entire city of Boston was shut down while local and federal law enforcement worked to identify and locate the bombers. This was unprecedented and was considered by some to be excessive given the scale of the attack. After all, while the Boston Marathon bombings were tragic, they killed far fewer people than the attacks on September 11, and they were carried out on a much smaller scale.

In this book, we will examine the events leading up to and following the bombings, the attacks themselves, and the history of the Tsarnaev brothers, as well as the aftermath of the incident and the role it has played in the United States's fight against terrorism.

CHAPTER ONE

Born on the Run

The Tsarnaev family story begins when young Anzor Tsarnaev's family was deported from their home in Chechnya to a forced resettlement camp in Tokmok, Kyrgyzstan, in 1944. Many Chechens were forced from their homes under the order of Joseph Stalin, the leader of the Soviet Union at the time. Because of the beliefs established under Russian communism, religious practices were aggressively discouraged, and Anzor's family was not able to practice their religion. When exiled

The Tsarnaev brothers' mother, Zubeidat, responded with anger over the police pursuit of her sons following the bombings.

Chechens were released and allowed to return to Chechnya in the early 1950s, the family stayed behind in Kyrgyzstan.

While serving in the Soviet military, Anzor met his wife, Zubeidat, who was from Dagestan, a republic governed by Russia. In 1986, during his service, Anzor's first son, Tamerlan, was born. Shortly after, the family moved back to Kyrgyzstan. Following the collapse of the Soviet Union in the early nineties, they moved to Chechnya, where Anzor had not been since he was a small child. As war between Russia and Chechnya loomed, the Tsarnaevs fled back to Kyrgyzstan until after the war.

But the homeland of Anzor's family was not the same. Following a long history of destabilization and conflict, Chechnya was now run by warlords with no central governing body. Dzhokhar and Tamerlan lived in their

LIFE DURING THE COLD WAR

The Soviet Union was a collection of states unified under a central government that was formed following the Russian Revolution of 1917. That was the year the Bolshevik Party, under the leadership of Vladimir Lenin, took control of what was the Russian Empire.

The Bolsheviks were strongly influenced by the political and economic ideas of Karl Marx, including his belief that religion was a tool of oppression by the state. "Religion is the sigh of the oppressed creature," he wrote, "the heart of a heartless world, and the soul of soulless conditions. It is the opium of the people."

Religious communities of all faiths had a hard time under Soviet rule. Anti-Semitism against Jewish people became even more common. Christian churches faced strong opposition. As the Soviets took control of countries in Europe and Asia, cultures that had been predominantly Buddhist or Muslim found their religions outlawed and their places of worship often destroyed.

For people who still believed, passing as atheist became a matter of survival. Some groups were able to practice their faith in secret, but many simply gave up on their culture. Others, especially in Muslim countries, attempted to organize retaliation with various degrees of success. During the Cold War between the Soviet Union and the United States, a number of these resistance groups came to be viewed as "freedom fighters" in the West because of their opposition to Soviet communism. However, many of those same groups went on to oppose and attack the Western military powers and would become rebranded as "terrorists," even though some of them had earlier received training and supplies from Western governments themselves.

ancestral land for only six months before they were moved again to their mother's homeland in the republic of Dagestan.

The Land of Opportunities

Meanwhile, across the ocean, Anzor's brothers were having a different experience in exile. Ruslan and Alvi Tsarni had moved to Montgomery Village in Maryland and found success; Ruslan had even become a successful corporate lawyer. In his communications with his brother, Ruslan spoke glowingly of his adopted home. For Anzor, who had become victim to violence from Russian soldiers and mobsters, it seemed that America was the best chance for his family's safety.

RUSSIA AND CHECHNYA

The conflicts between Russia and Chechnya have gone on for centuries. Despite countless regime changes, the two cultural groups have continued to clash formally since at least the late eighteenth century. For most of that time, the conflict could be viewed through the lens of Russian imperialism versus Chechen Islamic nationalism. Chechnya is a largely Muslim population, and Chechens resented being governed by outside, non-Muslim forces.

In recent decades, the conflicts have escalated severely. When Islamic insurgents based in Chechnya invaded Dagestan in 1999, the Russian government responded by invading Chechnya and placing it under occupation.

As a result of the destabilization of Chechnya, various warlords and insurgent groups have grabbed power throughout much of the country. Both sides in the conflict have committed atrocities against civilians in each other's country. With Russia having no interest in an independent Chechnya, and no centralized Chechen government to negotiate with, a resolution between the two will take a long time.

Claiming anti-Chechen discrimination, the Tsarnaev family applied for amnesty. They were permitted to immigrate to the United States in 2002. At the time, it was very uncommon for Chechens to move to the United States, and there were only about two hundred Chechen immigrants living there, largely in and around Boston. Most of them had come over only recently to escape the second war between Chechnya and Russia, so there was no real Chechen-American community waiting for them.

The Massachusetts Institute of Technology is one of the oldest colleges in America.

After arriving in New Jersey, the Tsarnaevs ultimately settled in Cambridge, Massachusetts, a city located right next to Boston that is home to two famous universities, the Massachusetts Institute of Technology and Harvard University. The family would eventually become lawful permanent residents, meaning they were allowed to stay in the country indefinitely.

Even though they had moved around a lot before arriving in America, it was a very different world for the Tsarnaevs. As a child, Tamerlan was terrified of the fireworks on holidays and special occasions; the loud noises and flashes were too similar to the bombs bursting in the air during the Russo-Chechen conflicts. Growing up, he tried to improve his English by reading the Sherlock Holmes stories by Arthur Conan Doyle, but the old-fashioned writing only confused him further.

As a teenager, Tamerlan was encouraged by his parents to study boxing. Martial arts like wrestling were very profitable back in the Caucasus. He won several awards and trophies, but he stopped for a few years to attend college part-time. Although the sport gave him a goal and a way to meet people, he admitted in a 2009 magazine interview that he didn't have any American friends. By 2011, Tamerlan had stopped boxing and drifted between delivering pizza and illegally selling marijuana.

The family's first decade in America was difficult. Their federal benefits were often cut and then restarted. Because the family had never been very religious, they felt isolated from the few other Chechen families who practiced Islam. After giving up on trying to have a boxing career, Tamerlan began studying the Quran with his mother as a way to try and connect with other Chechens. Anzor remained unobservant, while Dzhokhar was spending a lot of time with people from his high school.

Although a good student, teachers had noticed for some time that Dzhokhar was eager to please others and that he often told people what he thought they wanted to hear. As the only Chechen in his school, he began telling people he was Russian instead; no one even knew where Chechnya was. He joined the wrestling team and eventually made captain. But, like his brother, he also began to deal marijuana, and he began using it as well.

Meanwhile, Tamerlan was becoming more and more influenced by political conspiracies, both from Islamic extremists and American radicals, while conducting his Islamic studies. These conspiracies ranged from the belief that the September 11 terrorist attacks were staged by the American government to anti-Semitic paranoia about a worldwide Jewish conspiracy. This was the start of Tamerlan's extremist beliefs.

RUSSIA

DAGESTAN

CHECHNYA

BARDINO BALKARIA

INGUSHETIA

NORTH OSSETIA

GEORGIA

enokumsk

Chernyy Rynok

Achikulak

Kizlyar

Prokhladnyy

Mozdok

Malgobek

Groznyy

Khasav"yurt

Beslan

Nazran

Alagir

Vladikavkaz

Terek

Assa

Argun

Terek

Botlikh

P'asanauri

The conflict between Russia and Chechnya goes back centuries and may not be resolved for a long time still.

In 2012, Tamerlan flew to Dagestan, where he met with family he hadn't seen since he was a little boy. Being in a predominantly Muslim country that was no stranger to violent military attacks, Tamerlan found sympathetic ears for some of his ideas. He wanted to remain in Dagestan, but his American passport permitted him only a three-month visa. However, dressed in his American clothes and boasting about his boxing victories, Tamerlan stood out from the culture he hoped would embrace him. A distant cousin to Tamerlan told him to forget the struggles in Dagestan, follow a path of nonviolence, and return home to the United States. Tamerlan seemed to take this last suggestion seriously, as he returned to Cambridge only to become even more vocal about his increasingly extreme Islamic beliefs.

CHAPTER TWO

The Longest-Running Long Run

Marathon running is one of the oldest sports still practiced today. The name comes from the town of Marathon in Greece, where a major battle was fought in 490 BCE between the defending

The first marathon runner was Philppides, who is commemorated in

Greeks and the invading Persians. A famous legend says that after the Persians were defeated, a man named Philippides ran 26 miles (42 km) from the battlefield to the city of Athens to report the Greek victory.

The first Boston Marathon was held in 1897. Members of the Boston Athletic Association (BAA) had begun planning it the previous year.

PATRIOTS' DAY

Since it was first created, the Boston Marathon has always been held on Patriots' Day. This holiday in April commemorates the battles in Concord and Lexington in 1775 that began the Revolutionary War between colonial Americans and the British Empire. The colony of Boston had been under direct occupation by the British since 1768. Suspecting that local militias had been preparing for a rebellion, British soldiers were dispatched from Boston to apprehend insurgents in the town of Concord. Paul Revere and other riders famously rode out to warn colonists. After a brief conflict in Lexington, the British and colonial forces engaged in full battle at Concord, where colonial forces successfully repelled the British.

Patriots' Day is a state holiday, celebrated in Massachusetts and Maine with a three-day weekend. In addition to the marathon, the Boston Red Sox always play at home on this day, and there are historical reenactments of famous Revolutionary War battles. Especially in Boston, these reenactments help to connect modern-day Bostonians with their history. For residents of Massachusetts and Maine, the holiday is considered like a second July 4 celebration.

The holiday is also celebrated in Wisconsin and recognized in Florida.

Founded in 1887, the association encouraged participation in competitive sports and physical health.

The route of the first marathon was measured out by bicycle. To mimic the original Greek route of the first marathon, which stretched between Marathon and Athens, they wanted a variety in landscape, with hills as well as flat land. The route selected by athletic coach John Graham began in the town of Ashland and ran through five other towns before finishing in downtown Boston. Although Olympic athletes said that the course was very similar to the one in Greece, it was actually 1 mile (1.6 km) shorter than an actual marathon. Only seventeen men competed in the first event.

The Boston Marathon finish line: a site of victory turned tragic.

A New Tradition

Since then the marathon has been held every year, although the current route is a correct 26 miles (42 km). Only men were allowed to run at first, which was common at the time. Roberta Gibb was the first woman to run the marathon in 1966. When the BAA denied her application, she traveled from San Diego, California, and snuck into the race after it had begun. Women were officially allowed to run in the marathon in 1972. Today, the race also includes divisions for disabled runners, including wheelchair-bound and visually impaired athletes.

The modern-day race route begins in Hopkinton and continues through Ashland, Framingham, Natick, Wellesley, Newton, and Brookline, before finishing in Boston. Approximately 30,000 register to run the marathon every year. The runners come from countries all over the world, bringing friends and family with them to cheer them on. Many people come to the city to watch the race even if they don't know anyone who is participating.

PREPARING FOR A MARATHON

Marathons are major athletic events unlike almost any other. The preparation to run 26 miles (42 km) takes a long time, even for people who already run regularly. To train for a marathon, a person needs to gradually run longer and longer distances to develop physical and mental stamina. Most training programs suggest shortening a person's running distances in the weeks right before the marathon so as to not exhaust the body. It is also suggested to "cross-train," which means doing other forms of exercising such as biking or swimming to develop strength and stamina.

A balanced and healthy diet is equally important to prepare for running long distances.

Especially important during the final week before the event are foods like bread and pasta, which have lots of carbohydrates. These carbohydrates are stored in the body as glycogen, which the body converts into glucose to deliver energy. Runners have to learn how their level of exertion relates to their metabolism. If they push themselves too much early in the race, they risk burning too much glycogen too fast. By keeping a steady pace, they can keep their energy levels up for the whole run. But eating good foods with vitamins and minerals is also important for training to develop muscle and strong bones, and to stay mentally focused. Mental preparation is essential to running a marathon. Runners need to stay focused and alert, both to pay attention to their bodies and keep motivated to run such a long distance.

In 2015, the event brought in an estimated $180 million of revenue to the city. Over half of this amount is due to runners and visitors paying for hotel reservations and restaurant meals, entertainment and shopping, public transportation, and even souvenirs like newspapers. Other forms of revenue come from the media and event sponsors, and charity fundraising by participants. The Boston Athletic Association itself spends about ten million dollars on permits, security, and administration.

The marathon is such an important part of life in Boston—and such a point of pride—that many families in the area make it a tradition to see the race every year. This was the case for the Richard family, who would take their three children, including eight-year-old Martin Richard, to the finish line in order to cheer on the runners. Twenty-nine-year-old Krystle Campbell also enjoyed seeing the Boston Marathon every year since she was a girl, and she would also be standing at the finish line when the bomb went off.

CHAPTER THREE

Under Pressure

The life that Tamerlan Tsarnaev had returned to in Cambridge had changed. His parents had divorced, and shortly after he returned his mother moved back to Dagestan, where his father had also resettled. Dzhokhar wanted to move there as well. Although he himself was very critical of the American government, Tamerlan still wanted to get a valid US passport, as such a document would be very valuable internationally. When Dzhokhar returned to college, the once-crowded apartment felt sparse, with only Tamerlan, his wife, and their daughter.

Back at university, Dzhokhar's social circle was just as small. Though he had a small group of friends, Dzhokhar hardly spoke to his roommate, and most of his interactions with other students came because he had begun dealing marijuana out of his dorm room. While in high school, Dzhokhar had moved about between different social circles, but in college he never interacted outside of his small group.

Tamerlan found himself even more of an outsider, as his view of Islam was very different from that of the Muslims in the Cambridge and Boston area. His outspokenness against the imam in his local mosque led to him being removed. Most of his interactions with other Muslims came from Skype calls with friends back in Dagestan, who were leading lives very different from the one Tamerlan experienced.

Tamerlan Tsarnaev was once an accomplished boxer with Olympic aspirations.

Meanwhile, Dzhokhar's grades were slipping. In March 2013, Dzhokhar mentioned while eating with friends that he had learned how to make a bomb in his chemistry class. In the same conversation, he said that there were some passages in the Quran that he felt justified force. But his friends felt no reason to take any of this seriously; Dzhokhar was known for making random statements, and as far as any of them knew, he had no serious devotion to Islam.

Both Dzhokhar and Tamerlan began talking about retaliation for US involvement in Muslim countries, but none of their friends or family seemed to take them seriously.

TO THE SHORES OF TRIPOLI

The United States military has engaged with Muslim countries almost since its independence from Britain. In 1803, the US Marines were deployed in Morocco during the First Barbary War to rescue hostages from pirates. Following the terrorist attacks on the World Trade Center and the Pentagon in 2001, US forces were deployed to Afghanistan in an attempt to locate al-Qaeda leader Osama bin Laden. However, because of the mountainous and unfamiliar terrain, as well as the reluctance of locals to support American involvement, bin Laden would not be found and killed until 2011.

(continued on the page 25)

Al-Qaeda terrorists flew two hijacked planes into the World Trade Center towers on September 11, 2001.

(continued from page 23)

The US also launched an extensive ground war in Iraq in 2003 based on supposed intelligence that Iraqi dictator Saddam Hussein was harboring weapons of mass destruction. The weapons, if they ever existed, were never found, and the deposition of Saddam Hussein resulted in destabilizing the area and escalating conflicts between rival groups.

In addition to these large-scale actions, the American military has also been involved in Libya, Somalia, Yemen, and Pakistan. The US government has also been an ongoing military and political ally to the State of Israel, with which many Arab nations are in conflict.

Many people, Muslim and otherwise, see these actions as unjust and link them to escalating conflicts in these regions, with long-term consequences.

"Exactly": Improvised Explosive Devices

Exactly what preparations and discussions happened between Tamerlan and Dzhokhar before they carried out the bombing are uncertain. As the only survivor of the two accomplices, Dzhokhar's testimony is one of the only sources of information that law enforcement has. Other pieces of the puzzle came from interviews with friends and family members.

The bombs used during the marathon were made from pressure cookers, a type of kitchen appliance that uses steam within a sealed container to cook food quickly. According to Dzhokhar, the instructions for making such bombs were found in an al-Qaeda magazine called *Inspire*. *Inspire* was available online and was allegedly published by members of al-Qaeda based in Yemen as a propaganda and recruitment tool for their terrorist organization. Al-Qaeda used similar bombs in many of their

Summer 1431 | 2010

INSPIRE

« ...AND INSPIRE THE BELIEVERS »

Al-Malahem Media

Periodical Magazine issued by the al-Qà`idah Organization in the Arabian Peninsula

MAY OUR SOULS BE SACRIFICED FOR YOU!
SHAYKH ANWAR AL-`AWLAKĪ

The Tsarnaev brothers found the instructions for homemade bombs
in this al-Qaeda recruitment magazine.

attacks. These explosives, which are made from non-military materials, are called improvised explosive devices, or IEDs, and caused great destruction during the wars of Iraq and Afghanistan.

SUBMISSION AND THE BASE

It is important when reading about Islamic-related political and military issues to understand the difference between Islam and the organizations that claim to represent it.

The name "Islam" comes from the Arabic word *aslama*, meaning "submission." The central idea of Islam is submission to God, which is recognized in action by the five pillars of Islam: professing one's faith, saying five prayers daily, providing charity to those in need, fasting during the month of Ramadan, and going on a pilgrimage to the holy city of Mecca. There are no political or military actions required by these pillars to be a practicing Muslim.

The terrorist organization al-Qaeda, which means "the base," is an organization of Sunni Muslims, founded in the late 1980s by Osama bin Laden. Members of the organization had originally been trained to fight against Soviet military forces. Mostly known in America for their attacks against the US and its allies, the group has also fought against other Muslim groups, especially Shia Muslims in Iraq.

Both al-Qaeda and other Islamic terrorist groups, such as the Taliban, have attacked Muslims they believe are not correct in their faith and actions, and a majority of Muslims in the world have condemned the actions of both groups.

Earlier in the year, Dzhokhar had purchased a large amount of fireworks in New Hampshire. Some of these were set off on an outing with friends. The fireworks in question were large and not legal to possess in Massachusetts. Later, Dzhokhar would use the explosive powder from the fireworks he had not set off to build the bombs used in the Boston Marathon attacks.

During his interrogation after being captured, Dzhokhar said that Tamerlan was the one behind the plan. Interviews and testimonies by people who knew Dzhokhar seem to support this, and many reports and writings on the bombers have suggested that Dzhokhar's involvement may have been less the actions of a militant Islamist and more that of a lonely younger brother trying to please the older brother he admired. But whatever his motivations, Dzhokhar either did not try or was unable to convince his brother to abort this course of action, and he willingly participated in the attack. He also did not appear to show any remorse after he was captured for his role in them.

CHAPTER FOUR

...And They're Off

On the morning of April 15, 2013, the last preparations before the marathon were being finalized. Over the previous few days, roads had been prepared for closure and bus routes had been changed to avoid the route. Temporary structures like fences, refreshment

Taken shortly before the first of the bombs detonated, Dzhokhar is visible in a white hat next to the tree on the left.

stations, and portable toilets were set up in advance. On the morning of the race, officials were busy making sure all of the electronic equipment was working correctly and that race security and medical staff were on duty and had all their equipment. They were also checking in the tens of thousands of runners.

Timekeeping is critical at athletic events like these. Course clocks would have been set up all along the route, telling participants how much time had passed since the start of the race. These clocks all need to be exactly synchronized, and many running events will hire a company just to manage timekeeping. Some of these companies provide chips fastened to the runners' bibs that can digitally log their times as they cross checkpoints.

A Sad Start

The race began on a sad note, with twenty-six seconds of silence held in memory of the twenty children and six teachers who had died the previous fall in the shooting at Sandy Hook Elementary School in Newtown, Connecticut. At exactly 9:17 a.m., the fifty-two competitors in the wheelchair division were given their start.

The next two groups to leave the starting line were the women's elite runners at 9:30 and the men's elite runners at 10:00. In marathons, elites are considered world-class athletes who train at Olympic levels. Over a hundred women and men qualified as elites in 2013. After the men's elites left the starting line, the remaining registered participants were released over the next forty minutes in three different groupings.

The first runner to finish, with a time of two hours, twenty-six minutes, and twenty-five seconds, was Kenyan Rita Jeptoo. Less than four minutes before noon she crossed the finish line; seconds later she was

Rita Jeptoo of Kenya was the first to finish the 2013 Boston Marathon. She also won the Chicago Marathon that same year.

followed by Meseret Hailu from Ethiopia, and then Sharon Cherop, also from Kenya. The first of the elite men to finish was Ethiopian Lelisa Desisa with a time of two hours, ten minutes, and twenty-two seconds. Placing second and third after him was Kenyan Micah Kogo and Ethiopian Gebregziabher Gebremariam.

During this time, the Tsarnaevs, with their homemade bombs concealed in backpacks, would have begun moving into position. With thick crowds, closed roads, and rerouted public transportation, it would have taken them longer than usual to reach their target. Because of this, it is difficult to guess what time they actually planned to set off the explosives.

THE WOMEN AND MEN OF EMERGENCY SERVICES

Putting on an event at the scale of the Boston Marathon is a major task, requiring lots of coordination between different services.

Medical staff, including emergency medical technicians, ambulance drivers, and specialists in sports medicine, need to be on hand throughout the race route. Because of the changes to street traffic, an ambulance ride to the hospital might take longer than normal, so treating injured or ailing runners quickly and efficiently is important. Commonly expected situations would include dehydration and malnourishment, sprains and dislocations, or trip and fall accidents. Depending on the severity, these could merely cut into a runner's time or take them out of the race altogether.

Fire department services would have had extra planning in place to account not only for the changes of accessibility to get fire trucks to an emergency but also for the large increase of people in public places. These plans would also account for a larger number of people who may have disabilities or limited English language skills, making an evacuation even more complicated.

Finally, an event like this requires a large police presence for security and crowd control, and to assist fire and medical services if need be. For an event of this scale, both city and state police would be on hand and would need a system of communication and command for them to work together efficiently.

At 2:49 p.m. the first of the bombs detonated close to the finish line on Boylston Street. Seconds later, the other homemade explosive went off a block away in front of a restaurant. By this time in the race, the people running would not have been the elite, world-class athletes but ordinary people, some of them running in their first ever marathon. The bystanders were a mix of local Bostonians, out-of-town guests, and international visitors. Two hundred and eighty-two people were injured from the explosions and the ensuing chaos. The bombs took the lives of three people: Krystle Marie Campbell, a twenty-nine-year-old restaurant manager from the nearby town of Medford; Lu Lingzi, a twenty-three-year-old graduate student at Boston University, originally from Shenyang, China; and Martin William Richard, an eight-year-old boy from Boston. All three of the victims were standing close to the bomb when it detonated and suffered traumatic injuries before their deaths at the scene.

Heroes of Boston

Emergency services immediately went into action after the bombs detonated. With so many people on the streets, they tried to preserve the crime scene for investigation, attended to the wounded and injured, controlled the panicking crowds, and made an initial attempt to catch whoever had set off the bombs. It was an epic undertaking.

Over the next few hours, as no further attacks were carried out, media speculation began. At 4:28 p.m., the *New York Times* claimed that twelve people had been killed and that a twenty-year-old Saudi national was in custody. An hour later, *NBC News* claimed that a possible suspect was under guard in a hospital. Both of these claims were false and were quickly refuted by the Boston police commissioner.

City, state, and federal law enforcement worked together to investigate the attack and apprehend the bombers.

Shortly after 6 p.m., President Barack Obama made a statement about the attack, addressing what actions were being taken. Referring to the misinformation in the news and fear about the scope of the attack, he said: "We still do not know who did this or why. And people shouldn't jump to conclusions before we have all the facts. But make no mistake—we will get to the bottom of this. And we will find out who did this; we'll find out why they did this. Any responsible individuals, any responsible groups will feel the full weight of justice."

Among all of the news outlets and social media speculation, there was only one post that night from someone who knew exactly what had happened. Dzhokhar Tsarnaev tweeted: "Ain't no love in the heart of the city, stay safe people"

CHAPTER FIVE

Nowhere Left to Run

With the crime isolated to the two bombings, law enforcement could begin to investigate. After tallying the number of casualties and making sure the city was secure, more than one thousand officers and investigators from city, state, and federal agencies began working to identify and locate the terrorists.

One of the victims of the attack was Jeff Bauman, a twenty-seven year old who had come to the race to cheer on his girlfriend, Erin Hurley. Seconds before the bomb detonated, he saw Tamerlan, and the young man struck him as odd.

"[It] was a dense crowd and … he kind of nudged me and I looked back at him," Bauman said during his testimony. "And that's when I looked at him and he just looked very suspicious. You know, he didn't look like anybody that was there. He was alone; he wasn't … watching the race, he wasn't—you know, it didn't look like he was having fun like everybody else. Everybody else there was clapping, watching the race [and] talking to each other. And … I looked at him and he kind of stared down at me and … I just thought it was odd."

Bauman had noticed the backpack that Tamerlan had dropped on the street, and while it struck him as unusual, he didn't recognize it as a threat. Moments later, the bomb went off right next to him. When he came

Jeff Bauman was cheering on his girlfriend at the finish line when the bombs went off; he lost his legs in the attack but was able to identify Tamerlan Tsarnaev while still in the hospital.

to, Bauman's left leg was damaged beyond repair below the knee, and the bomb had taken his right leg off. He was taken to Boston Medical Center where doctors worked to keep him from dying due to blood loss.

When he came to after emergency surgery, Bauman was able to give a description of Tamerlan, a major step in identifying the attackers. The police now had an idea of who to look for in security recordings.

One of the most time-consuming parts of the investigation involved looking through videos and still pictures taken by security cameras throughout the city. If they could find pictures of the bombers and match up the timestamps on the digital recordings, they could attempt to track their movements, where they had come from, and where they were going.

Meanwhile, forensic scientists examined the materials from the bomb to determine what the bombs had been made of. Depending on what those materials were, this information could help piece together where and when the bombs had been made. Federal Bureau of Investigation (FBI) analysts identified the materials used in the bombs as coming from pressure cookers that had been packed with nails, shrapnel, and other materials.

A Picture Is Worth a Thousand Words

On April 18, the FBI found video taken from security cameras that showed Tamerlan and Dzhokhar, although they did not yet know who they were. They released these images to the public in the hopes that someone would recognize them and come forward.

Sure enough, back at Dartmouth, Dzhokhar's roommates saw the pictures of the bombers and thought one of them look like their friend. When they texted him about it, he replied that they shouldn't text him any more and if there was anything they needed from his dorm room to go and take it. In the room, they found a backpack containing fireworks with the explosive powder removed and his laptop. From reports on CNN, it was becoming more certain that Dzhokhar was one of the bombers. Panicking, they threw the backpack and computer in a school dumpster, where it was later recovered by FBI agents.

The Tsarnaev brothers' path of destruction wasn't over, though. That night at about 10:30 p.m., a police officer was shot dead while on patrol on the MIT campus. Twenty-seven-year-old Sean Colier was found in his police car. The brothers had attempted to steal his gun while fleeing, which resulted in his death.

Shortly after the shooting, Tamerlan hijacked a car and its driver, forcing him to drive the brothers around the city in order to withdraw money from ATMs.

Security camera footage was invaluable in identifying Dzhokhar and

The driver was able to escape at a gas station in Cambridge and call the police. Because his cellphone was still in the car, it could be tracked by its signal. The brothers were located in the nearby suburb of Watertown. Police tried to apprehend them, and the brothers retaliated with gunfire and thrown explosives. In the shootout, one officer was injured and Tamerlan was shot multiple times. Dzhokhar escaped in the stolen vehicle, driving straight through the police and accidentally hitting his brother. Tamerlan was taken to a nearby hospital, but the doctors were unable to save him. He died that night.

THE DEPARTMENT OF HOMELAND SECURITY

Formed in 2003 as a response to the terrorist attacks on September 11, 2001, the Department of Homeland Security (DHS) works to prevent and manage terrorism by foreign operatives on American soil. It is a cabinet department, similar to the Department of Defense (DOJ), and it is able to operate domestically without following the same procedures and protocols of conventional law enforcement. Several government agencies are now under the authority of DHS, including Immigration and Naturalization Services (INS), the US Coast Guard, the Secret Service, the Transportation Security Administration (TSA), and others. The department has faced criticism for violating the civil liberties of American citizens, as well as for a lack of transparency in regard to its operations and budget.

But Dzhokhar was still on the run. At the time, law enforcement still had no idea whether the brothers had been working alone or with accomplices, or whether there were any more attacks planned. To find out the extent of what could have been a full-blown terrorist cell, and to bring him to justice for the four dead and hundreds injured, Dzhokhar could not be allowed to escape Boston.

Lockdown

On April 19, the city of Boston issued a shelter-in-place order. At a news conference, a city official announced that residents of the city and nearby towns were to stay indoors, and businesses were told not to open. Automated phone calls and social media posts also went out to warn residents to stay indoors. Public transportation was closed for the day; no buses or taxis would run and the subway stations were locked up. Amtrak service in and out of Boston was suspended and the area was made a no-fly zone. Harvard and the Massachusetts Institute of Technology, as well as all local public schools, closed for the day. In Watertown, where Dzhokhar had last been seen, police officers from the Special Weapons and Tactics unit patrolled the streets and guarded key locations.

Despite the manhunt, Dzhokhar remained at large. Massachusetts governor Deval Patrick received a call from the president. While supportive, he told Governor Patrick that the lockdown couldn't go on indefinitely, and the governor agreed. Shortly after 6 p.m., the lockdown was lifted by Governor Patrick.

With the lockdown over, the people of Boston and the neighboring towns were able to go to the store or return to work. Public transportation started back up again. Many residents were relieved to get out of the house, although many also remained fearful.

Governor Patrick knew that the shelter-in-place order could not be held indefinitely.

Around this time, Watertown resident David Henneberry went out to his backyard where he had his motorboat stored. From an upstairs window in his home, he had noticed something amiss during the shelter-in-place order. The material used to cover the 24-foot (7-meter) motorboat to protect it when not in use looked askew. Large pieces of hard plastic that were used to protect the sides of the boat were lying on the ground. A strong storm could have knocked them loose, but the weather had been clear.

Henneberry walked over and cautiously looked under the sheeting. The plastic made the interior dark and shadowy, but the late afternoon sunlight

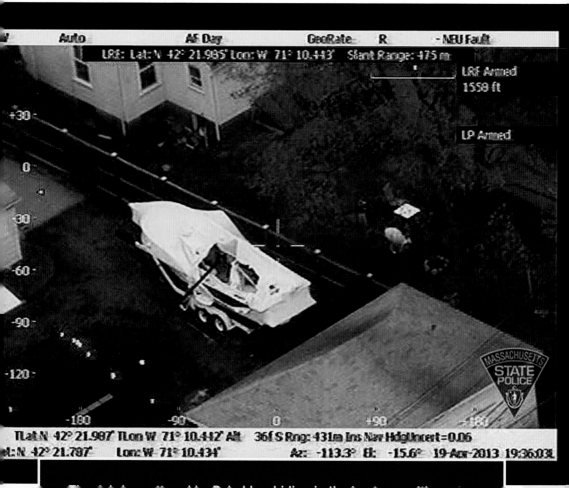

that came through the gap revealed dark smears on the interior. They were bloodstains, and looking further in, he could see a form that could have been a body.

Having abandoned the stolen vehicle and bleeding from the wound he received during the gunfight with the police, Dzhokhar Tsarnaev had climbed into the boat during the previous night. He had remained in hiding there for eighteen hours.

Henneberry immediately went back into the house and called 911. Police forces surrounded the boat, preparing for what could have been a violent standoff. After three hours, Dzhokhar finally gave himself up and was taken into custody and treated for his wound. Inside the boat, he had written a note on the wall saying that he and his brother had committed the bombings in retaliation for American military action in Muslim countries.

CHAPTER SIX

Finishing Time

With Dzhokhar captured and Tamerlan dead, the case was closed on the Boston Marathon bombings. There was no terrorist cell, no links to al-Qaeda or any other extremist group. The responsibility for the 4 dead and 264 wounded fell to two young men acting on their own.

Several of Dzhokhar's friends from Dartmouth were interrogated by federal agents. Because of the permissions given to law enforcement investigating terrorist attacks, they were held and questioned without legal counsel present. Almost all of them admitted they knew nothing about the attack, but under his fourth questioning Dzhokhar's friend Robel Phillipos admitted to being involved in the removal and disposal of the evidence from the dorm room. For lying to federal agents, he was sentenced to three years imprisonment.

Controversies also arose following the attack. In August 2013, *Rolling Stone* magazine did a feature article on the Tsarnaev brothers and the attack. A picture of Dzhokhar from before the bombings was used on the cover, and many people found it disturbing to have a terrorist bomber portrayed in an attractive light. The magazine was accused of glamorizing the killers, which prompted the following response from the editors: "The fact that Dzhokhar Tsarnaev is young,

and in the same age group as many of our readers, makes it all the more important for us to examine the complexities of this issue and gain a more complete understanding of how a tragedy like this happens."

Two years later, a full report was released on the official response to the bombings. The authors of the report found that some of the measures taken by officials following the attack were successful. Because of the coordination already in place between city and statewide police, as well as emergency services, during the marathon, Boston was exceptionally well equipped to respond to the disaster. This allowed officials to share resources and information to both investigate and pursue the bombers as well as to care for the wounded and protect residents and visitors.

AN OVERREACTION?

In both the domestic and foreign press, journalists questioned the government's response to the bombings. Had the authorities overreacted in placing Boston and the neighboring towns under lockdown? Michael Cohen, writing for the British newspaper the *Guardian* pointed out that residents of London had been subjected to worse and more frequent terrorist attacks—often with both military-grade and homemade explosives, as in the Boston attack—for decades without having to shut down the city. However, Nate Rawlings of *Time* magazine pointed out that shelter-in-place orders have been issued many times before, and for a variety of reasons, such as during the 2003 severe acute respiratory syndrome (SARS) epidemic in Toronto.

The report's authors also found that the decision to close businesses and services and keep residents indoors was justified. The report confirmed that, with the known information at the time, this was the best possible decision to protect people. The lockdown had been discussed and confirmed among all levels of government and law enforcement from the start of the shelter-in-place order until the capture of Dzhokhar Tsarnaev.

However, the report also found that while the general organization of law enforcement was a success, individual officers were unprepared. During both the Watertown shootout that resulted in the death of Tamerlan and the standoff with Dzhokhar in the boat, officers were found to have lacked "weapon discipline." The report said of the Watertown shootout with the brothers: "Although initial responding officers practiced appropriate weapons discipline while they were engaged in the firefight with the suspects, additional officers arriving on scene near the conclusion of the firefight fired weapons toward the vicinity of the suspects, without necessarily having identified and lined up their target or appropriately aimed their weapons."

Among the chaos, damage, and injury caused by the bombings, there was also the matter of the race itself. The runners who were still in the marathon when the bombs went off were obviously unable to finish. This was a huge disappointment for them, not only due to the sacrifices they made during their training but because they had missed the opportunity to finish the marathon and might not qualify for it again. To make up for this, the Boston Athletic Association promised that all runners who didn't finish because of the bombings would be guaranteed registration for the 2014 marathon.

For the one-year anniversary of the bombings, the victims were remembered and honored by many across Boston.

Not Forgotten

For the one-year anniversary of the attack, the president of the United States recognized a moment of silence honoring those who died in the attack. President Obama stated, "Today, we recognize the incredible courage and leadership of so many Bostonians in the wake of unspeakable tragedy. And we offer our deepest gratitude to the courageous firefighters, police officers, medical professionals, runners and spectators who, in an instant, displayed the spirit Boston was built on—perseverance, freedom and love."

The trial against Dzhokhar Tsarnaev began on March 5, 2015. Previously, US attorney general Eric Holder had announced that the federal government would be seeking the death penalty against him. The trial lasted a little longer than a month, and there was no doubt that, based on the evidence presented, Tsarnaev was guilty. Jeff Bauman took the witness stand to state that he saw one of the brothers placing a backpack on the ground just before it exploded. Victims and family members of victims testified about what they saw and the pain they went through following the attack. Martin Richard's parents testified about their own injuries as well as the loss of their son. But the Richards also asked that Tsarnaev not receive the death penalty, as they said it would only increase their anguish.

On April 8, 2015, Dzhokhar Tsarnaev was found guilty of all thirty charges against him; he was later sentenced to death. Each use of a weapon or explosive was given multiple charges. For example, just one of the two bombs made from pressure cookers carried the following charges:

> "[The] use of a weapon of mass destruction, resulting in death; and aiding and abetting; possession and use of a firearm during and in relation to a crime of violence, resulting in death; and aiding and abetting; bombing of a place of public use, resulting in death; aiding and abetting; possession and use of a firearm during and in relation to a crime of violence, resulting in death; aiding and abetting; malicious destruction of property by means of an explosive, resulting in death; aiding and abetting; possession and use of a firearm during and in relation to a crime of violence, resulting in death; aiding and abetting."

In addition to charges specific to the use of weapons and explosives, he was also charged with conspiracy to use a weapon of mass destruction, resulting in death; conspiracy to maliciously destroy property, resulting in

This artist's sketch of Dzhokhar during his trial was made available for journalists. Cameras were not permitted inside the courtroom.

death; carjacking resulting in serious bodily injury; and interference with commerce by threats and violence.

At the time of this writing, Dzhokhar Tsarnaev is awaiting execution in a high-security prison in Florence, Colorado. Just before being sentenced to death, he apologized for his role in the bombings. He turned to the victims and their families and told them, "I am sorry for the lives that I've taken, for the suffering that I've caused you, for the damage that I've done. Irreparable damage."

It's true—the damage the Tsarnaev brothers inflicted can never be undone. The Boston Marathon continues to commemorate the victims of the 2013 bombings.

Timeline

▶ **1897** The first Boston Marathon is held on Patriots' Day.

▶ **1986** Tamerlan Tsarnaev is born in the former Soviet Union.

▶ **1993** Dzhokhar Tsarnaev is born in Kyrgyzstan.

▶ **1994** The Russo-Chechen war begins.

▶ **1996** The Russo-Chechen war ends.

▶ **1999–2002** The Tsarnaevs live in Dagestan during this period.

▶ **2001** On September 11, 2001, terrorists hijack four planes in the United States and use them to carry out attacks against the World Trade Center and the Pentagon, killing 2,996; the war in Afghanistan begins in October and will last until 2014.

▶ **2002** The Tsarnaevs move to the United States.

▶ **2003** The Iraq War begins; it will last until 2011.

▶ **2006–2008** Tamerlan attends Bunker Hill Community College before dropping out.

▶ **2008** Tamerlan begins to show signs of more extreme religious belief; he stops drinking and smoking.

▶ **2011** Anzor and Zubeidat Tsarnaev file for divorce; Dzhokhar enrolls at the University of Massachusetts at Dartmouth.

▶ **2012** From January to July, Tamerlan spends time in Dagestan, visiting his family.

2013 Dzhokhar and Tamerlan set off bombs at the Boston Marathon on April 15; on April 19, Tamerlan dies in the early morning after a police shootout, while Dzhokhar is captured later that day.

2014 US attorney general Eric Holder states that the federal government will seek the death penalty against Dzhokhar.

2015 On June 24, Dzhokhar is found guilty on thirty criminal charges and is sentenced to death.

Glossary

anti-Semitic Prejudiced beliefs against people of Jewish faith and/ or heritage.

atheist Someone who does not believe in God or does not follow any particular religious beliefs.

Chechnya A central Asian republic of Russia's, which is predominantly Muslim.

course clock Timekeeping device used to track running time during a race.

Department of Homeland Security (DHS) The American government agency created to share intelligence and enforce anti-terrorism laws in the wake of the September 11 terrorist attacks.

Federal Bureau of Investigation (FBI) The highest ranking domestic law enforcement agency in America.

glycogen A type of carbohydrate that the body converts into energy.

improvised explosive device (IED) A type of bomb made out of non-military materials.

lawful permanent resident Someone who is not an American citizen who has been granted permission to live and work in the United States.

lockdown A state of isolation or restricted movement during an emergency for security purposes.

marathon A race, originating from Greece, which takes place over 26 miles (42 km).

marijuana An herbal drug derived from the leaves of the cannabis plant.

Patriots' Day A state holiday celebrated in Massachusetts and Maine, commemorating the battles that began the American Revolution.

pressure cooker A kitchen appliance that uses contained steam heat to cook food quickly.

al-Qaeda An Islamic terrorist organization, originally based in Afghanistan.

Quran The holy text of the Islamic faith, believed to be the word of God as dictated to the prophet Muhammad.

retaliation Revenge, or harming someone else because you feel that person has unjustly harmed you.

shelter-in-place An order given during an emergency to take shelter in the place where someone already is, rather than evacuating.

Special Weapons and Tactics (SWAT) Law enforcement units trained in military-level equipment and methods.

Taliban A political movement based in Islamic fundamentalism, which was in power in Afghanistan from 1996 until 2001.

Boston Athletic Association (BAA)
185 Dartmouth Street
Boston, MA 02116
(617) 236-1652
Website: http://www.baa.org
The Boston Athletic Association (BAA) is a nonprofit sports organization for the city of Boston and its surrounding areas.

Boston Police Headquarters
1 Schroeder Plaza
Boston, MA 02120
(617) 343-4500
Website: http://bpdnews.com
The Boston Police Headquarters is the main office for the Boston police department.

Federal Bureau of Investigation (FBI)
Department of Justice
935 Pennsylvania Avenue NW
Washington, DC 20535
(202) 324-3000
Website: http://fbi.gov
The FBI is a federal law enforcement and domestic intelligence agency that investigates national criminal activities.

US Department of Homeland Security (DHS)
12th and C Street SW

Washington, DC 20024

(202) 282-8000

Website: https://www.dhs.gov

The Department of Homeland Security was created in the wake of the
September 11 attacks and is tasked with providing a coordinated
response to potential terrorist threats against the United States.

US Department of Justice (DOJ)

950 Pennsylvania Avenue NW

Washington, DC 20530

(202) 353-1555

Website: http://www.usdoj.gov

The US Department of Justice is the government department that oversees
law enforcement and justice administration in the United States.

US Department of State (DOS)

2201 C Street NW

Washington, DC 20520

(202) 647-4000

Website: http://www.state.gov

The US Department of State is an executive department that advises the
president and government on foreign policy.

Websites

Because of the changing nature of internet links, Rosen Publishing has
developed an online list of websites related to the subject of this book. This
site is updated regularly. Please use this link to access the list:

http://www.rosenlinks.com/TER21/marathon

For Further Reading

Bauman, Jeff, with Bret Witter. *Stronger*. New York, NY: Grand Central Publishing, 2014.

Bergen, Peter. *United States of Jihad: Who Are America's Homegrown Terrorists, and How Do We Stop Them?* New York, NY: Broadway Books, 2017.

Bodden, Valerie. *The Boston Marathon Bombing* (Surviving Disaster). Edina, MN: ABDO Publishing, 2014.

Challen, Paul. *Surviving the Boston Marathon Bombing*. New York, NY: Rosen Central, 2016.

Cooper, Alison. *Facts About Islam* (World Religions). New York, NY: Rosen Central, 2011.

Gessen, Masha. *The Brothers: The Road to an American Tragedy*. New York, NY: Riverhead Books, 2015.

Hayurst, Chrisa. *Ultra Marathon Running* (Ultra Sports). New York, NY: Rosen Central, 2002.

Helman, Scott, and Jenna Russell. *Long Mile Home: Boston Under Attack, the City's Courageous Recovery, and the Epic Hunt for Justice*. New York, NY: New American Library, 2015.

McPhee, Michele R. *Maximum Harm: The Tsarnaev Brothers, The FBI, and the Road to the Marathon Bombing*. Lebanon, NH: ForeEdge, 2017.

Philpott, Don. *Understanding the Department of Homeland Security*. London, UK: Bernan Press, 2015.

Seely, Robert. *The Russo-Chechen Conflict 1800-2000: A Deadly Embrace*. New York, NY: Frank Cass Publishers, 2001.

Sherman, Casey. *Boston Strong: A City's Triumph Over Tragedy*. Lebanon, NH: ForeEdge, 2015.

Streissguth, Tom. *The Security Agencies of the United States: How the CIA, FBI, NSA, and Homeland Security Keep Us Safe* (Constitution and the United States Government). New York, NY: Enslow Publishing, 2012.

Whitewell, Stephen. *The Battles of Lexington and Concord: First Shots of the American Revolution* (Spotlight on American History). New York, NY: Powerkids Press, 2016.

Williams, Brian Glyn. *Inferno in Chechnya: The Russian-Chechen Wars, the Al Qaeda Myth, and the Boston Marathon Bombings.* Lebanon, NH: ForeEdge, 2015.

Bibliography

Active Network. "How to Plan a Marathon: 20 Steps for 26.2 Race Directors." *Active Network: Endurance*, 2015. http://www. activeendurance.com/resources/event-director-guides /how-to-organize-a-marathon.

Bauman, Jeff, with Bret Witter. *Stronger*. New York, NY: Grand Central Publishing, 2014.

Gessen, Masha. *The Brothers: The Road to an American Tragedy*. New York, NY: Riverhead Books, 2015.

Higdon, Hal. *Boston: A Century of Running*. Emmaus, PA: Rodale Press, 1995.

Lowery, Wesley. "7 Key Takeaways from the Long-Awaited Boston Marathon Bombing Report." *Washington Post*, April 3, 2015. https:// www.washingtonpost.com/news/post-nation/wp/2015/04/03/7-key -takeaways-from-the-long-awaited-boston-marathon-bombing-report.

Massachusetts Emergency Management Agency. *After Action Report for the Response to the 2013 Boston Marathon Bombings*. December 2014. http://www.mass.gov/eopss/docs/mema/after-action-report-for -the-response-to-the-2013-boston-marathon-bombings.pdf.

Morrison, Sara, and Ellen O'Leary. "Timeline of Boston Marathon Bombing Events." Boston.com. Retrieved November 2016. https://www.boston .com/news/local-news/2015/01/05/timeline-of-boston -marathon-bombing-events.

Reitman, Janet. "Jahar's World." *Rolling Stone*, July 17, 2013. http://www .rollingstone.com/culture/news/jahars-world-20130717.

United States District Court of Massachusetts. "United States v. Dzhokhar A. Tsarnaev, Defendant." January 15, 2016. http://www.mad.uscourts .gov/training/pdf/09517236471opinion%20and%20order%20tsarnaev.pdf.

Van Allen, Jennifer, Bart Yasso, and Amby Burfoot. *The Runner's World Big Book of Marathon and Half-Marathon Training.* Emmaus, PA: Rodale Press, 2012.

Williams, Bryan Glyn. *Inferno in Chechnya: The Russian-Chechen Wars, the Al Qaeda Myth, and the Boston Marathon Bombings.* Lebanon, NH: ForeEdge, 2015.

Index

About the Author

Greg Baldino holds a bachelor of arts in fiction writing from Columbia College Chicago, where he studied genre literature and twentieth-century social history. He is the author of *Art, Technology, and Language Across the Middle East* and a contributor to the collection *War: The Human Cost*. He lives in Chicago in a converted carriage barn with a vagabond pigeon.

Photo Credits